CHALLENG

DANG
AT SL

David Orme

CONTENTS

Introduction

Imagine you are on a sunny beach. The sea is blue and sparkling, and seems safe. And yet it is one of the most dangerous places on earth. Ships can be wrecked by storms or dangerous rocks. Swimmers can be swept away by fast currents.

People love the danger and excitement of the sea. Yachtsmen sail long distances in the world's most dangerous oceans. Divers risk death with every dive. There are brave people whose job it is to risk danger to help others …

This book tells the story of some of these people.

Villains

of the sea

Pirates!

Imagine you are a sailor on a **merchant ship** in the early eighteenth century. You are leaving America with a rich **cargo**.

Suddenly there is a yell from the **crow's nest**.

"It's Blackbeard!"

Blackbeard was the most feared pirate of all time. If he captured your ship you had two choices: you joined his crew on his ship, the *Queen Anne's Revenge* – or you **walked the plank**!

Blackbeard's real name was Edward Teach. He was cruel even to his own crew. But he met his match when he was shot dead in a sea battle in 1819.

Wreckers!

Imagine that you are the captain of a ship. You are somewhere near the coast of Cornwall, 200 years ago. If only you could see the light from the lighthouse, you would know where you are!

Then you see a light! That must be the harbour! You sail in to shore. Suddenly you find your ship is smashing onto rocks! There is no harbour. The wreckers have tricked you.

Wreckers were men who lit fires to confuse ships and wreck them so they could steal the cargo. If the sailors were killed, that was just too bad ... the wreckers didn't care!

Heroes of the sea

Ellen MacArthur

On 5 November 2000, 24-year-old Ellen MacArthur started the challenge of her life. A solo race in her yacht, *Kingfisher*, would take her 24,000 miles around the world!

In the ninety-four days of Ellen's race she:

- woke up just in time to steer away from an iceberg;
- struck an underwater object and damaged the ship's hull – which she fixed!
- climbed to the top of the mast in a storm to free the sail.

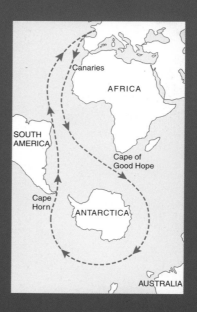

On 11 February 2001, Ellen arrived back in France. She was second in the race. She was the youngest woman ever to have sailed around the world!

Grace Darling

Grace Darling's father was a lighthouse keeper. He was the keeper of the Longstone Lighthouse in the north of England. At dawn on 7 September 1838, Grace and her father woke to a storm. They could see a ship in trouble a mile out to sea.

Twenty-two-year-old Grace begged her father to try to rescue the sailors. They struggled through the waves in their small rowing boat. They reached the wreck at last. Grace stayed on the wreck while Mr Darling took five sailors back to the lighthouse. He then came back and rescued Grace and the other men.

Air sea rescue

You can see the ship below you. It is sinking fast. There are four men on board ...

"Lower away!"

The **winch man** lowers you down. At last you reach the men. One is injured. He will need a stretcher. The others can be winched up with a **harness**.

The men, cold and frightened, are wrapped in blankets. The helicopter heads for home. Below, the ship is sinking. Without you, they would all have drowned ...

14

Captain Webb and Alison Streeter

It was Wednesday, 25 August 1875. Captain Matthew Webb stepped out of the sea on to a French beach. He had left Dover the day before and had been swimming for nearly twenty-two hours. He was the first person to swim the English Channel.

Today, Alison Streeter is the cross-channel heroine. She has swum the channel over thirty times. She has even swum one way, turned around and come back!

People are trying longer and longer sea swims. In some places they even use safety cages to avoid been eaten by sharks!

GREAT EXPLORERS

Columbus reaches America

Christopher Columbus lived from 1451–1506. At this time many people thought that the world was flat. Columbus was sure it was round so he decided to sail all the way around the world to reach India. In 1492 he set off to cross the Atlantic. People said, "That man Columbus is mad! Just wait till he gets to the end of the world. He'll fall off!"

When the food and water began to run out, the crew became frightened. Perhaps they would fall off the end of the world!

At last Columbus reached some islands. He thought he had reached India, so he called them the 'West Indies'.

He did not know that he had discovered a new continent. Even when he died, he did not know that he had reached America.

Captain Cook

Captain Cook lived from 1728–1779. He was probably the greatest sea explorer of all time.

In 1768 he set off in the *Endeavour*. He crossed the Atlantic and sailed round **Cape Horn**, which was a very dangerous journey. He crossed the Pacific and reached Australia, which was an unknown land. By the time he got back to England, he had travelled right around the world. It had taken him three years.

In 1779 Cook was on another expedition. This time his luck ran out. The natives in Hawaii were not friendly. Cook was killed in a fight.

Wreck divers

Diving on wrecks is exciting, but it can be dangerous!

Swimming around outside a wreck is interesting and quite safe, but many divers are tempted to go inside …

It will be dark in the wreck and the water won't be clear. If it is an old wreck, parts of it may fall on you. Your **SCUBA** gear might get tangled, trapping you ...

So, don't be tempted unless you know what you are doing, and always have a **buddy** with you.

Remember, the sea is a dangerous place ...

Disasters

Titanic

"Iceberg – dead ahead!"

Passengers on the *Titanic* did not know they were in danger. They did not know that there were not enough lifeboats for everyone. It was her first voyage.

On the night of 14 April 1912, the *Titanic* was sailing at full speed – even though the captain had been warned about icebergs. It was nearly midnight when the iceberg was spotted.

It was too late to steer away. The iceberg scraped along the side of the *Titanic*. Water poured in.

At twenty past two in the morning, the ship sank. Only 705 people were saved. Nearly 1500 people drowned in the freezing ocean.

Exxon Valdeez

On 24 March 1989, the oil tanker *Exxon Valdeez* sailed slowly out of Prince William Sound, Alaska. It was a tricky job. The captain decided to **change course** so the ship would not hit ice. He gave his orders, then he went to his cabin.

Half an hour later, the huge tanker hit a **reef**. Over the next few days, 11 million gallons of oil poured into the water.

Alaska is a remote place and it was difficult to get clean-up teams there. Cleaning up the oil was very slow. Huge numbers of sea birds, animals and fish died. It was one of the worst oil spills ever.

The pride of the fleet

The *Mary Rose* and *Royal George* were two of the navy's
finest ships. Both sank near Portsmouth, and both
sinkings were an accident!

On 15 July 1545, Henry the Eighth came to see the *Mary
Rose* in a battle with the French. The ship was top-heavy
with guns. When the guns fired, the ship tipped over.
Water poured in through the **gun ports**. It quickly sank.

In 1782, the hull of the *Royal George* needed repairs. They moved the guns to one side of the ship. This would make the ship lean over so it would be easier to repair the hull. But the ship leaned over too far.

The *Mary Rose*

Escape from a submarine!

Imagine you are trapped in a submarine at the bottom
of the sea. Quickly you put on your **pressure suit**.
The **escape hatch** closes. Water pours in. You float
upwards, faster and faster. Will you make it to the
surface? Your chances are better now than they were
fifty years ago. But even then some people survived.

In 1941 the submarine *HMS Perseus* was sunk by a
mine. All sixty members of the crew died – all except
thirty-one-year-old John Capes. He said that it was the
rum he drank before leaving the submarine that helped
him to swim the 170 feet to the surface.

Fifty years later, divers found the Perseus. They also found
John's rum bottle!

Shark attack!

In 1937, a **pearl diver** called Iona Asai was attacked by a shark. It was a 10-metre-long tiger shark. The shark started to swallow the diver's head!

Quickly, Iona jabbed his fingers into the shark's eyes and squeezed. At last the shark let go.

The diver was rushed to hospital where shark's teeth were found in his neck!

Glossary

buddy diving partner

Cape Horn the most southerly point of South America

cargo goods carried by a ship

change course go in a different direction

crow's nest look-out place on the mast of a sailing ship

escape hatch door to get out of a submarine in an emergency

gun ports windows that cannons were fired through

harness straps put around a person who is to be lifted into a helicopter

merchant ship ship carrying goods

mine bomb used under water

pearl diver person who dives into the sea to find pearls in oysters

pressure suit special clothes to help you survive in deep water

reef dangerous rocks just under the surface of the water

SCUBA Self-Contained Underwater Breathing Apparatus – equipment to let you breathe under water

walk the plank a way in which pirates got rid of their victims – over the side!

winch man person operating the machine that lifts people up into a helicopter